Play Baseball

Trace Taylor

This is a baseball.

This is a baseball field.

These are baseball players.

pitcher

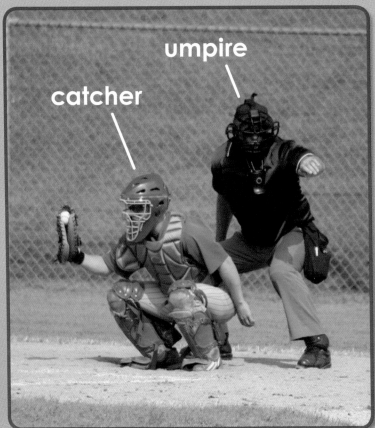

umpire

catcher

The players throw the baseball.

The players catch the baseball.

5

batter

The players hit the ball. They hit it with a bat.

Some players don't hit the ball.

bat

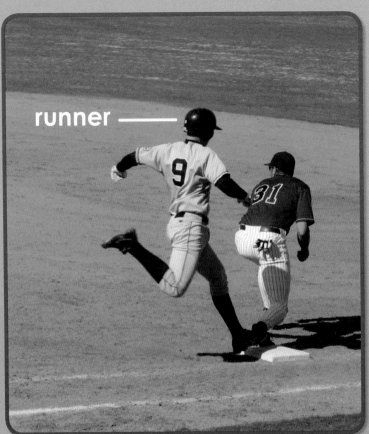

runner

Players who hit the ball have to run.

This is a base.

The player has to get to the base.

Some players slide in the dirt to get there.

Some players jump to get there.

This man will see if the play is good or bad.

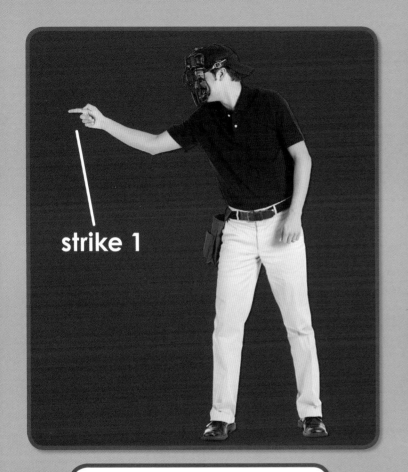

strike 1

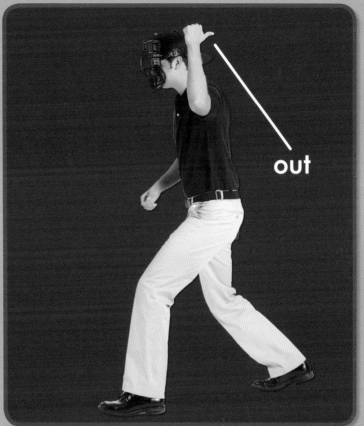

out

This man says you didn't hit the ball.

This man says you are out of here.

The Baseball

On game day, the umpire receives a box of new baseballs from the home team. Each box is sealed and certified by the league president. Before the balls are used in the game, each ball is rubbed with "magic mud" to remove its shine and make it less slippery. The mud was discovered by White Sox infielder Lena Blackburne in the 1930s. It was found along the Delaware River in New Jersey and has been used throughout the major and minor leagues ever since. Other methods have been tried to de-slick baseballs, but nothing works as well as Blackburne Baseball Rubbing Mud.

When the mud rubbing is done, the balls are taken out to the field, where each one is used for only 5 to 7 pitches. When a ball gets too dirty or scruffy, the umpire takes it out of the game and puts in another new ball. As many as 100 or more baseballs are used in one major league game.

Baseball Diamond

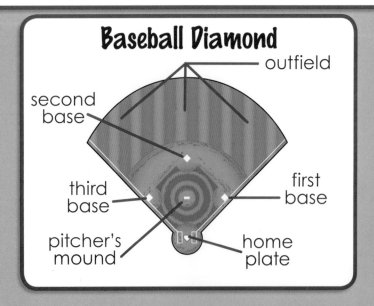

outfield

second base

first base

third base

pitcher's mound

home plate

Power Words

How many can you read?

a	has	it	says	this
are	have	jump	see	to
didn't	here	of	some	who
don't	if	or	the	will
get	in	out	there	with
good	is	play	these	you

Practice With College & Career Ready Standards

1. What was this book about? How do you know?

2. What position would you want to play in baseball? What would you have to do in that position? What in the pictures or words supports your answer?

3. Why would a player need to slide or jump to get on base? What in the pictures or words supports your answer?

For more information, please visit
www.americanreadingathome.com